Routledge Revivals

Festival Stories of Child Life in a Jewish Colony in Palestine

Festival Stories of Child Life in a Jewish Colony in Palestine

Hannah Trager

Routledge
Taylor & Francis Group
Routledge Revivals

First published by George Routledge & Sons Ltd.

This edition first published in 2018 by Routledge
2 Park Square, Milton Park, Abingdon, Oxon, OX14 4RN
and by Routledge
711 Third Avenue, New York, NY 10017

Routledge is an imprint of the Taylor & Francis Group, an informa business

Publisher's Note
The publisher has gone to great lengths to ensure the quality of this reprint but points out that some imperfections in the original copies may be apparent.

Disclaimer
The publisher has made every effort to trace copyright holders and welcomes correspondence from those they have been unable to contact.

A Library of Congress record exists under ISBN: 20021347

ISBN 13: 978-1-138-60429-2 (hbk)
ISBN 13: 978-1-138-60438-4 (pbk)
ISBN 13: 978-0-429-46231-3 (ebk)

Festival Stories of Child Life
in a
Jewish Colony in Palestine

Dedicated to

my dear and esteemed friend

Henrietta Lowy,

whose interest in the religious welfare of the young has stimulated me to write this work.

THE FOUR QUESTIONS AT THE SEDER

Festival Stories of Child Life in a Jewish Colony in Palestine

BY

HANNAH TRAGER

Author of

Stories of Child Life in a Jewish Colony in Palestine

WITH A PREFACE BY

THE VERY REVD. DR. HERTZ

CHIEF RABBI

ILLUSTRATED

LONDON:

GEORGE ROUTLEDGE & SONS, LTD.

NEW YORK: E. P. DUTTON & CO.

PREFACE

This little volume is a welcome addition to the small number of books of interest for Jewish children in English-speaking countries. The Festival stories are charming pictures of the life in the Jewish colonies in the pioneer days of the New Settlement in Palestine a generation ago. The human appeal of these tales is sure to give the Jewish child who reads them a deeper affection for the Sacred Occasions of the Jewish Year. Though living in the West, the child will feel itself linked to the Jewry in the Land of our Fathers—the Holy Land, which, by the help of God, is again to be the Homeland of a great portion of our People.

J. H. HERTZ.

Chanucah, 5680.
London.

CONTENTS

Festival Stories of Child Life

IN A

Jewish Colony in Palestine

A TALE OF THE PASSOVER

It is just one day before Passover. In every house women and girls and even the boys are busy hurrying and scurrying about.

In Palestine Passover is a very serious affair. Every house must not only be cleaned and scrubbed, but it must be whitewashed and new sand-floors made where there are no cobbled or marble floors. As Passover falls in Spring, and the weather is warm and generally dry, everything in the houses is carried out of doors. Clothes are hung up to air and be sunned on clothes-lines, and well shaken in case there may be some crumbs of bread or cake in the seams or linings. Even pockets are turned inside-out for the same reason.

To open every book is the most important

thing: they must be looked through, shaken, and clapped, in case crumbs had slipped in when the reader had been eating while reading, for many had only time to read or study when eating their meals. By those who keep the Law nothing is done in a half-hearted way; and as the Law said no leaven bread should be in any Israelite's house during the eight days of the Passover Festival, they keep strictly to the Law and collect all the leaven bread, cakes, and crumbs, and burn them on the eve of Passover.

What a joyful, happy time it is to the young folk, helping thoroughly to clean the house!—and, though it is often hard or heavy work, they always look upon the cleaning as play. When they carry the feather mattresses out of doors, they generally put one of the boys on each, roll it round him, and toss him over and over as if he were a barrel; or they may take a blanket, and four of the boys will hold the four corners while one boy gets into the middle of it; then they throw him up into the air. And what fun and laughter there is, until the mother or elder sister comes out to scold them for the noise they are making!

Even the tiny tots have their Passover work. They keep driving the fowls and ducks away from the furniture and the mattresses out of doors for a sunning, for the ducks and hens just love to make themselves comfy by settling down on something nice and soft.

Of all the festivals, the boys love the Passover most, for they then have most freedom and fun. What they all like best of all is, after everything is clean and tidy again, all the leaven bread cleaned away for the last time for eight days, when they see their mother go to the great trunk, uncover it, and then open it. In this trunk all the special silver, glass, and china is kept specially for the Passover Festival. These things are always more beautiful than those used at any other time of the year.

Everything connected with the Passover is good and beautiful, whether it is the silver, which the rich use, or the china and glass, which the poorer use. After every Passover each article is again carefully wrapped up and packed away until the next time this Feast of Freedom is to be celebrated; for nothing that can be afforded is thought too costly for the commemoration of this special occasion, when, after years of slavery in Egypt, the Jews became free men.

All the children stand round the mother, jumping with excitement and joy, and crying out, "Let's see, let's see! What's in this paper!" when each article is brought out, especially when they see the small silver or coloured glass goblets that belong to each child for the Passover Feast. Even the older ones take a great delight in seeing these things unpacked.

Joy, noise, and cheeriness was everywhere in the Colony in the year of which this story is written except in Shimon's house, for his mother was ill and his father was away looking for work. He was only a farm-labourer, and there was not much work for him to do during this season of the year. His brothers and sisters were too small to do anything towards preparing the Passover. Shimon tried hard to scrub the doors and wooden partitions of their rooms; but he could not manage to do much as he was neither big nor strong. At last he sat down outside on the doorstep and dropped his head on his knees, and cried from weariness and disappointment.

Joseph just happened to pass by and saw the little lad. He said, "Hullo, Shimon! what's gone wrong with you?"

"It is not with me," said Shimon, crying; "but I feel awful bad. Just fancy, only one day before Passover, and my father's not back, and nothing has been turned out and cleaned, and *I* cannot manage to do it all."

Joseph's kind heart was touched at the little lad's sorrow, and said: "Never mind, Shimon, all will be done."

"But how?" said Shimon. "Do you think

a miracle will happen and Angels will come down and whitewash the room ? "

" Well, I don't know," said Joseph, " but all is possible with God ; for did not He perform a miracle, when—after He had caused the Jews to mark their houses by a blood-token to distinguish them from the houses of the Egyptians in order that the bad Angel should ' pass over ' them so that no plague should fall upon them—Did He not divide the Red Sea for the Israelites to pass through ?—and so He has still power to perform a miracle and do in your home all that ought to be done, before Passover begins.

Surely His hand is not shortened ?

Don't give way, Shimon, put your trust in God " ; and he left him saying those words.

Joseph did not stop with simply saying those words. He knew that God works through human agents. So he went to Abraham, Moses and Mandel and told them of Shimon's trouble. They put their heads together and decided on a plan ; but they felt they must take their mothers into their confidence. So each boy went home and told his mother what he thought of doing. Then each boy returned, and they all went together to Shimon's house, and said to him : " Look here, Shimon, you must take on yourself the responsibility of a man, for your mother is ill with malaria and in a high fever, so you cannot ask her advice. Do what has to be done before Pesach."

"What can I do?" asked Shimon.

"Well," Moses said, "we've thought of a plan. My mother has sent you a loan of money, and a waggon is starting for Jaffa in fifteen minutes. So you had better go to Jaffa. Buy some new utensils for the Passover, and some matzos, for you know they cannot be bought here, and your father may return without the matzos."

Shimon thanked them gratefully, for he knew that they were right, and at any cost matzos and new utensils must be had. So he rushed off to the waggon that was going to Jaffa.

Meanwhile the boys had decided that, while Shimon was away, they would whitewash and do all the necessary cleaning, for the boys were quite as handy as the girls. In a few minutes they were busy, one carrying a pail of lime, another a brush, and the other a pail of sand, and so on.

The furniture was all put outside; but one thing puzzled them—how could they whitewash the ceiling when Shimon's mother was delirious and too ill to be moved? Then a bright idea came to Abraham, and he said: "Let's call in the girls to help us. Let's put a sheet over the back of the bed and let the girls hold it up over the bed like a tent and so cover Shimon's mother and the bed, while that part of the ceiling is being whitewashed."

No sooner said than done. The boys rushed out and got their sisters to help them, and the girls just loved taking part in helping when they knew the reason.

Then the boys got on to a table and began the whitewashing. Of course it was not as nicely done as it would have been had a man done it, and when they saw some parts rather smeary they said: "Well, it's *clean*, at any rate."

Then they did the other work, and were so interested in trying to finish it all before Shimon came home that they quite forgot their meals.

When it was near sunset all was finished, and with what pride and pleasure did they give a last look at the result of all their work, before returning home! The ceiling and walls, which had looked nearly black, were now nice and white. The floor, as well as the chairs and table and other wood-work, had been well scrubbed with white sand. Even the porch looked clean. Oh, how delighted they were to think of the lovely surprise it would be to poor Shimon, and how God could even now-a-days perform miracles, even if He did do so through human beings; for does not the idea or good thought that enters the mind come from God, and is it not quite as much a miracle as when He divided the Red Sea ? Thus they reasoned.

The girls, by the way, determined not to be outdone by the boys. So one girl remained with Shimon's sick mother, and gave her cooling drinks, and dipped some linen into vinegar and water and laid it fresh from time to time on the poor woman's head. This refreshed her so much that in a few hours the fever left her, and she fell into a calm, restful sleep.

Meanwhile, the others went home and each returned with something that was necessary for Passover, which they hid away in the cupboard in Shimon's home.

Knowing Shimon's father would be coming home for certain that night so as to clean away the leaven, and there was no one to prepare it for him, they put some crumbs of bread in the different corners of the room, and at one corner they placed a wooden spoon and a few large feathers tied together, for him to brush all the crumbs into the spoon (according to the Law the *man* must clean his house of all the impurities, and then burn every bit of bread, even the crumbs, on Passover eve).

One girl remained in the house till Shimon returned from Jaffa, and she had not long to wait.

When Shimon saw the place all clean and even whitewashed, he uttered an exclamation of surprise, and asked the girl whoever had done it all. She said she could not say, but perhaps it was Elijah who had come and had done it, for it was an ancient saying that Elijah always came and helped those who hoped in God when they needed help, especially before Passover.

The boy looked very puzzled, for he knew that it must have been some living person ; and that, as the girl would not tell him, he would have to find it out in some other way.

Just as he was going to see some of the boys to ask them if they knew, his father arrived, dragging his feet from sheer weariness and quite bent down through carrying only a small bag of potatoes which a neighbour had given him. It was not so much the weight of the bag that bent him down, as the load of care and worry. He had found no work and it was almost too late to prepare properly for Passover.

" Where is mother ? " he exclaimed.

" Mother has malaria, and is laid up in bed," said Shimon.

" Oh, my God ! " moaned the father, and sank down into the nearest chair. " Is not my cup of misery full yet ? Here we are, on the eve of Passover, and not a thing in the house, no matzos, no wine for the Hagadah, and not even money to buy the necessary utensils!"; and he dropped his head into his hands.

Shimon went up to him and said: "Father, don't grieve, God has not forsaken us. Just look round and see what God has done for us."

Then he told his father how sad and discouraged he, too, had felt in the morning in not having the cleaning done and money to buy the necessary things; and how Moses's mother kindly sent him a loan of money, and advised him to go into Jaffa by a cart just leaving, to buy the things; and how while he was away all the cleaning had been done and his mother become much better—and that he had no idea by whom it had all been done.

The father lifted up his head and said: "Yes, my son, we must always trust in the Lord, for He is our help in time of trouble. At least we have the necessities for Passover. God be thanked for it. He will not forsake us!" He got up then quite cheerfully and went to the bed to see how his wife was, and, when he saw how peacefully she was sleeping, he knew the fever had left her.

"Come, children," he said, "let us clear away the chometz." So he lighted a candle, took the wooden spoon and feathers, said a prayer, and brushed the crumbs into the spoon, and

Shimon and the younger children followed him from corner to corner, till all the crumbs were brushed up.

Next morning, in the centre of the Colony a bonfire was made, and every boy and girl brought the chometz from their various homes wrapped up in a piece of rag and threw it on to the bonfire.

In going Shimon met the boys and told them about the room being cleaned, etc., and asked them if they knew who had done it. They said: "No, we cannot say," for they meant to keep it a secret, for boys and girls like nothing better than a secret, only they can't keep one long.

Shimon returned home after burning the chometz, still puzzled but happy, for his mother was better, and he hoped they would now have a pleasant seder, although there was not much to eat; but still they had matzos, the bitter herbs, and charoses to dip it in. The charoses is made of apples, nuts, dates, wine, and cinnamon, and looks like mortar, and the parsley and bitter herbs are dipped into it, so as to remind us of the mortar that our forefathers were forced to make in Egypt. The bitter herbs are to remind us of the bitterness of our forefathers' lives while slaves in Egypt.

Then Shimon helped his mother to tidy herself for the occasion, as she was too weak to sit up.

She was moved onto a couch, and he jokingly said: "Mother, dear, to-night, not only will father have a hasebah (that means reclining on a couch with pillows while saying Hagadah) but you will have a reclining couch, and so it should be," and he added laughingly, "for if father is a king to-night, you are the queen."

"But not much of a kingdom have we, my son, for it's poverty that stares us in the face," she said weakly.

"Oh! yes we have," answered Shimon. "Did not King Solomon say: 'He is rich who is contented,' and surely, mother dear, we are all contented and happy to see you better and able to celebrate the Feast of Freedom with us to-night, even if it is only with matzos and herbs; and, as we dip the bitter herbs into the charoses, let us remember that the bitterness is mixed with sweetness, and it will always be a lesson for us to remember how lovingly God has dealt with us, His children."

The mother smiled to hear the wisdom of her son, for nothing gives greater joy to a Jewish mother than to see how learned in the Law her children are.

She gave a sigh, and said: "You are wise, my son; you have given me a lesson too. Yes, King David was right when he said we could learn wisdom from the young. Go, my son, and wash the children and yourself and get ready to go to the synagogue."

So Shimon went off to do as he was told, and the mother fell into a quiet sleep again.

Meanwhile, one of the girls who had helped to clean the house had been keeping watch to see when all was clear, and, seeing Shimon and the rest of the family start for the baths, she peeped through the window : seeing the mother asleep, she rushed back to her friends, who were ready and carrying the things their mothers had prepared for them. So they opened the door softly, and as they were barefooted very little noise was made. They spread the table with a white cloth that they had brought with them ; put the candlesticks with candles in the middle of the table ; then laid a glass round for each member of the family ; a bottle of wine and the soup and fowl and knaydlich they put into the cupboard ; and then quietly left the room on tip-toe, and hid themselves behind the back door, where there was a small window through which they could look without being noticed, just to see the surprise of Shimon's family when they returned.

It needed some patience, for Shimon and his brothers did not return from the bath for some time ; but the girls did not mind that, for they sat chatting and imagining what each one would say when he saw it all. At last their patience was rewarded by the shout of surprise they heard, which told them that they must be back. Then they peeped through the window, and what a joy it was to them to see the faces of real pleasure and surprise.

The shout awoke Shimon's mother, and they all ran round her to kiss and hug the poor mother, who was weeping for joy. Then they heard another exclamation, and the girls knew it came when Shimon opened the cupboard and they saw all the good things there for the feast.

So our girls went home feeling very happy, to tell their mothers and the boys what joy was in Shimon's home.

In the evening, on returning from synagogue, Shimon's father put the table near the couch so that the mother could take part in the saying of the hagadah, and they celebrated that Feast of Freedom and performed the seder as they never did before. Every word they uttered was a thanksgiving to God for His goodness to them, and blessings were given for those beings who had provided their needs; and so with much gladness they said Hallel and ate the bitter herbs. Although they felt in their mouths the bitterness, their hearts were full of sweetness towards God and men. Even the afikomen was not forgotten, but enjoyed by the children.

LAG B'OMER

LAG B'OMER

LAG B'OMER fell on a cloudless day in the month of May. The sky was blue, as only those who have visited Palestine know it can be. The early morning air was fresh and fragrant with the scent of flowers, when streams of young and old from Jerusalem trudged along with happy faces, each carrying a basket of gaily-coloured 'kerchiefs tied up by the four corners filled with good things for the Feast Day. The children ran, skipped, or sang, as cheerily as the birds, out of real joy of heart.

All were hurrying to secure a shady spot under the fine olive and cedar trees which grew near Rabbi Shimon's tomb, in a meadow a short distance out of the suburb of Meah Shorim. The tomb had been built over the Rabbi's grave in the form of a small ancient house like "Mother Rachel's Tomb."

Rabbi Motel and thirty boys from his chedar were amongst the holiday-makers, and they were lucky to get some ground for their feast under a shady olive.

This Rabbi was a gentle old man, very different from many of the Rabbis of earlier days: for he never beat his boys, and yet they felt a few words of reproach from him far more keenly than other boys would have felt a beating from another Rabbi, less gentle.

When all were comfortably rested, the boys asked him to tell the tale of Bar Kochba and Rabbi Akiba, and others, knowing this, came too and formed a circle round him to hear him speak.

He told them that Lag B'omer meant the 33rd day of the Omer, which we in England know as the month of May.

The Omer (a *measure* of barley) 49 days, Passover to Pentecost.

Some historians say that the 33rd day of the Omer was chosen as the Feast Day in memory of Bar Kochba and the wise and patriotic Rabbi Akiba, because in 134 c.e. a great plague suddenly ended. Other historians say this date was chosen because on that day in the same year none of Rabbi Akiba's pupils was killed, though a battle was raging between our people and their Roman oppressors.

Between 132 and 134 c.e. both Bar Kochba and Rabbi Akiba helped their people who still remained in Judea to free themselves from their Roman conquerors. Since the taking of Jerusalem in 70 c.e., when the Temple was burnt, the Romans had oppressed the remaining Jews so terribly, that Rabbi Akiba's spirit burned within him, in pity for his afflicted people ; and, having great confidence that Bar Kochba would prove to be a great wise general, he sent his pupils throughout Judea to arouse his people to prepare in secret to free themselves.

For two years Bar Kochba with his Jewish army, through their bravery and bold attacks, were so successful that for a short time Judea was again ruled by a Jewish government. But finally a Samaritan spy betrayed Bar Kochba, when defending his greatest stronghold, the city of Bethar, where he fell, and Rabbi Akiba was taken prisoner and tortured till he died, calmly smiling at his torturers with the Shema on his lips, having said just before that he rejoiced that he was permitted to show his love for his God and nation by dying for them. After describing a few more incidents connected with the history of these two great men, Rabbi Motel ended, and his boys quickly laid out on a cloth all the good things their parents had given them for the Feast, and they counted the minutes till they could begin to eat, for how their mouths watered when they saw the fowls, pastries, cakes, nuts, large tomatoes, and fruit ! But try to imagine their disappointment when the Rabbi said :

" Well, boys, our feast does indeed look tempting ; but before we begin where is the water to wash our hands with ? "

Each boy looked questioningly at the others, and what was their dismay when they found that not one of them had remembered to bring water for the washing of the hands, and of course, no good orthodox Jew would eat with unwashed hands or without giving thanks to God for their food. Inwardly they thought: " Must this Feast Day become a Fast Day ? "—to fast when they were so hungry, and with such delicious-looking food within sight and reach, would be far harder than fasting on the usual Fast Days; but, however hard it was, they could not commit such a sin as to eat without washing their hands, especially as the Rabbi was there!

Suddenly they heard an Arab calling out: " Drinks! drinks! Only a farthing a cup! "

Sholem said: " I have a few pence, so will buy some cups of water."

The other boys jumped up, and those who had some pence said they would buy some too.

Their hopes, however, were soon dashed to the ground, for the Rabbi said: " We cannot use that water, boys; for other things will be mixed with it."

When they heard this they began to feel very sad, and they asked the Rabbi if they could drink some of the wine or water or syrup that they had brought with them. As there is no Law against drinking with unwashed hands, the

Rabbi gladly consented, and, when they had emptied a bottle, they felt refreshed and much brighter, and determined to make another effort to find the much-needed water. So they decided to divide into two parties and see what each could do. One party went from group to group of holiday-makers and asked if they would sell them any water they had to spare.

In those days pure water was very scarce in Palestine. Even in Jerusalem it was so precious that people did their best not to waste any; for, after the Spring rains, no rain fell again to fill their cisterns till the autumn. Now, thank God, it is different, for since the deliverance of Jerusalem one of the first acts of our deliverers was to make a good water supply for the Holy City.

The holiday-makers on this hot day were not very keen to part with water; but, as the boys offered to buy it, they sold them a little, which they took back with great glee to the Rabbi, who said he would keep it in a shady spot till the other party returned.

Meanwhile the second party were told that very often near Rabbi Shimon's Tomb a man sold water; but that day no one could see the water-seller. Weary, thirsty, and disappointed, the lads sat down to rest in the shade of a small grotto near by, which had been formed between two large stones.

Sholem suddenly jumped up and, feeling his trousers, said: "Look, boys, my trousers are wet! There must be water here. Let's look."

After careful search, they found some water bubbling up as if from a spring; it ran past among some boulders and soon was lost to sight.

Their first thought was to run and tell their Rabbi. As they excitedly ran past the various groups of holiday-makers, the elderly people thought the boys were only up to some mischief or boyish pranks, which were always allowed on Lag B'omer.

When Rabbi Motel heard the good news, he and all the boys round him forgot their hunger and left all the good things laid out on the cloth, and ran off to see this unexpected sight. Others followed him, feeling there must, of course, be something worth seeing; quite a crowd gathered on the spot, and, when they saw the water bubbling up from the spring, they all cried out: "A miracle! a miracle!" for indeed it was a miracle in those days to see running water in Palestine.

When the excitement was over and all the questions answered by the boys as to how the water had been found, the Rabbi and they remembered their untouched feast, and hurried back, thankful that they had now enough water with which to wash their hands. Alas ! another disappointment was in store for them—they found that some Arabs had stolen all their dainty dishes, and had not even left the table-cloth.

In Palestine Jews are very generous and thoughtful, and, when this disappointment was known, those of the holiday-makers who had some food left generously gave some of it to the boys, so that the Rabbi and they had as much as they cared to eat.

Before saying grace, the Rabbi said : " My boys, by our many disappointments, you have proved, not only to yourselves, but unknowingly, no doubt, to those around you, how much self-control you possess ; for it is ever so much harder to fast on a Feast Day than on a Fast Day. All who have any commonsense avoid on Fast days, where possible, going within sight or scent of rich dainty foods, so that these senses may not be unnecessarily aroused. Non-Jews often laugh at us orthodox Jews for our strict observance of Ceremonial Laws, and I think it is our duty, when we have the chance, to help them to understand that God ordained them, as well as the great moral Laws, to help us to train our characters towards perfection, by cultivating various necessary virtues, and our Ceremonial Laws regarding eating and drinking are intended to teach us all the importance of cleanliness (which the old sages said was 'next to Godliness') and self-control.

"In Deuteronomy xxi. we are seriously warned against excess in eating or drinking, and in Proverbs xxiii. we are warned against making companions of those who do, for they will surely come to poverty.

"Besides self-control, you have shown us how cheerfully and unmurmuringly you took your disappointments. We know how severely God punished our forefathers for murmuring in the wilderness, for murmuring is a sign of lack of faith in God's Power, Wisdom, and Justice, to help guide or guard in time of need.

"Sholem, God has specially rewarded you to-day, as He did Hagar centuries ago, by guiding you to find the spring, which, owing to the dry porous ground around, has until now been hidden from sight. Now we hope wells may be dug near this spring, and the water will fill them so that it may be stored safely for times of need."

The Rabbi then said grace, and told them to go and join in the Lag B'omer games, with their bows and arrows; but many of the holiday-makers returned to the spring, and danced and sang, while others stood round in a circle, clapping their hands (for no instrument of music has been allowed to be used in Jerusalem since the temple was burnt in 70 c.e.).

Later on, some boys and girls wrote little notes asking the dead Rabbi to get some of their wishes granted, and then pushed them under the door of the Tomb whilst they repeated at the same time several psalms. Those in trouble did the same thing. Some broken-hearted men and women and even little children would stand and sob out their troubles and pray to the spirit of the saintly Rabbi to intercede for them. Boxes belonging to various charities in Palestine were hung around the tomb, and those who could dropped a few coins into them. Blind and ailing beggars also sat around, begging for alms.

A little way off, all was bustle and excitement, for the meadow was full of groups of young folks.

The boys who had bows and arrows and pop-guns played at soldiers, imitating scenes in the days when Palestine was under Roman rule. Sometimes they let off the pop-guns unexpectedly near people for sheer mischief. Then, of course, there was a scuffle and rush to try and catch the rogues, who usually escaped, as no one was very strict on Lag B'omer. After sunset, both old and young gathered in groups to recite the Evening Prayer, and then started home, tired but happy, with a good-bye word to each and a wish that they might all meet again the next year in the same spot.

PENTECOST:

OR

THE PILGRIMAGE

PENTECOST OR THE PILGRIMAGE

PASSOVER had come and gone, and the children were back in school for the first day after the holiday.

Lessons finished, the master called the boys round him and said: "Now, my boys, you did not enjoy this Passover less than other Passovers because I asked you all to give a little more thought to its meaning, did you?—or because we spent part of it in walking about together and talking it over?"

"No, no," cried the boys; "we understood it much better and enjoyed it more than any Passover we have spent yet."

And Moses, who was unlike the son of Amram, for he spoke very easily, put up a hand and said: "Please, teacher, can I say something?"

"What is it, Moses?"

"We should like you to tell us how to spend each of the Festivals as we never spent it before."

Said the master: "I will certainly do my best to meet your wishes. The next Festival will be Pentecost. But, before we go on to that, I should like to hear from you what you learned about Passover. Would you like Moses to be your spokesman, or shall it be another boy ?"

"Moses shall be our spokesman," decided the boys, with one accord.

Moses flushed with pleasure, and began: "In Egypt our people were treated very harshly —they were slaves; they had to work, without being paid, from early in the morning till late at night, and drivers stood over them with whips. But God had mercy on them and led them out of the country . . . if I told you everything it would take too long," said Moses, pausing to take breath.

"All right," said the teacher, smiling; "tell us what is most important; but not too fast! —we are not in such a hurry, and we like listening. So the children of Israel were set free ?"

"Yes," continued Moses; "but they were not yet really free. They were free only in their bodies, because they could not be made to toil any more, making bricks and being beaten; but they were not free in their souls— they were not yet good at all, for no sooner were they safely out of Egypt than they began to grumble and to wish themselves back. They forgot all they had had to suffer there, and thought only of the good things they had had to eat."

At this all the boys laughed.

"Yes," said the teacher, "so it was. They did not understand that freedom is more precious than anything else, and, though Moses told them that the God of their fathers had brought them out of Egypt to be His own people, they knew nothing about Him as yet. What did they make, Moses, to worship instead of God?"

"A Golden Calf," said Moses; "the women and girls gave their gold earrings to be melted down, and the people said the calf had saved them—and Moses was very angry with them."

"Yes," said the teacher, "and tell me, you little Moses of Pethach Tikvah, what do we call such a thing as the Golden Calf, which the foolish Israelites worshipped?"

"An idol."

"Right. Do people worship idols now?"

"No, teacher—I mean not the Jews."

"Don't be too sure," said the teacher. "There are all sorts of idols! There is an idol called Money, and an idol called Rank, and even an idol called Learning, that is when a person learns and learns and does no good with what he knows, but only wants to be thought clever. However, we will talk about these things another day. Now, when did the Children of Israel begin to be really free? When did they begin to understand that there are better things than a good dinner? When did they learn that they had souls as well as bodies, and that their souls too were to live a free, new, and beautiful life? Think a minute, Moses, and remember what we said."

Moses thought a little, and then he looked at the teacher and replied: "When they heard the Law! And then it was Pentecost."

"That was it," said the teacher; "and now, boys, listen: Just before the end of Sefirah, two days before Pentecost, each of you shall tell me what he has found in himself good enough to deserve a reward. Be very honest with yourselves, and, if you don't find much, try to make it a little more. What the reward will be is my secret!"

All through Sefirah the boys were in great excitement. There was no need to remind them that Sefirah means the counting, for they did nothing but count the days to Pentecost.

Two days before the Festival, the master, who had not mentioned the matter again so that sometimes they wondered if he had perhaps forgotten, called to them and said: "Well, my boys, the moment has come for the reward! But who is here to claim it? How many of you have found some good in yourselves?" And as nobody could make up his mind to speak first, he added: "Step forward, Moses, and tell me what you found that is good?"

Moses, somewhat abashed, stepped forward, and said: "I found some good and also some bad. I like to know my lessons and to do a kind thing and to speak the truth, but I don't always like to go to school or to pray when it is a very fine day."

"And you, Joseph, come forward and stand beside Moses."

Joseph did as he was told, and said: "I don't always like to do errands for my mother when I come home from school, but all this time I tried to do them without grumbling, and now I don't mind nearly so much—and I mean to go on trying and then perhaps I shall not mind at all."

"Abraham," called out the teacher; "you next."

Abraham came forward and fixed his beautiful eyes on the teacher's face. "Well," said the teacher, "you are not all goodness, are you?"

"I think," said Abraham, "that I am mostly badness."

"No, teacher, no," cried the others, afraid lest Abraham should lose the reward; "it's not true! He has a lot of badness, but he has just as much goodness, and we should not care for any reward unless he had one too, because he never has anything nice without letting us all share."

"I see," said the teacher. "Who comes next? Dan . . ."

So it went on till it came to Chaim, the dunce. There was great curiosity to hear what Chaim would have to say for himself. Presently it turned out that he had nothing to say at all, because the effort of thinking himself over had been too much for him.

"What is to be done?" asked the teacher, gravely; "if Chaim has not found any good in himself, how can he, Chaim, take a part in my reward?"

The boys had felt inclined to make fun of Chaim, but he stood there looking so stupid and so sad that pity came over them and a very curious thing happened: the same idea came to them all, and, before anybody had spoken a word, Moses held up a hand.

"Yes Moses?" said the master.

"We are sorry for Chaim, and we each give him a little tiny bit of our reward."

"Good!" said the teacher; "I am satisfied, and Chaim, too, shall go up to Jerusalem for the Festival."

For two seconds the boys were dumbfounded; then a cry burst forth "To Jerusalem! We are going to Jerusalem!"

"Why, yes," said the kind master, looking quite as happy as his pupils. "You know that in old days the men and boys (those boys were a little older than you, but never mind) went up three times a year, when possible, to worship in the Temple. There is no temple now, but there is no reason why we should not go to our beautiful city, and thank God that we, at least, are again living in our own country. And, if we cannot make any gifts to the Temple, we can always make the offering of a glad and thankful heart."

Then the master unfolded his plan. The boys were to ask their parents for some provisions for the way, and to meet him at dawn outside the school.

That evening the boys nearly drove their mothers and sisters mad over the getting ready. True, their parents had known of the plan for some time, and had been preparing the food—hard-boiled eggs (the small Eastern eggs, but very nice), cheese, home-made cake, dried figs, and also vegetables and chickens for the poor people in Jerusalem. So there was really no need for any fuss. But nothing would persuade the boys that things would be ready in time—they were even afraid to go to bed lest they should wake too late, and some of them dropped asleep as they were, done-up with excitement, and were carried to bed afterwards.

Meantime, there was great heart-burning

among the girls, for whom no such delightful plan had been made. A few went about weeping and refused to work, and they all decided that it was most unfair. They went to the same school as the boys; they also were Jewish children; and the Festivals were surely there for them too.

At last a few of the fathers, who were going to Jerusalem on horses, arranged to take a girl each on his horse, and the others resolved that when the next Festival came round, they would all find a way to go.

Next morning, just as the last star or two went out in the sky, the party moved off on horses and donkeys, some on foot with mules carrying the food in panniers, and the whole of the rest of the Colony was there to see them start.

Just as day began to dawn, they reached Ramleh, where there is now a railway station, but in those days there was no railway. Here the riders got down, and they all sat under some very old and very big olive-trees with great twisted grey trunks and knotted roots, and had breakfast.

After this they travelled on till it became really hot, and then they settled down under some more trees for a few hours till the heat should pass off. There was no hurry about getting anywhere before night, for they would be able to journey on by the light of the moon.

The older little boys, who had walked most of the way, were very tired, though too happy to mind, and they lay down and went to sleep.

The girls, on the other hand, had been riding and were quite fresh, and they unpacked and started getting dinner ready. One of the men rode off to an Arab village near by, and brought back water, live charcoal, and milk, so they were even able to make coffee, and when the boys awoke, behold a white cloth laid under a tree and a tempting meal. Then the boys were glad that some girls had come too, as they had made themselves so useful; and they washed their hands, said grace, and enjoyed themselves.

The sun was still too high for them to start, so the boys asked their master to tell them something to beguile the time, and he opened a Prayer Book and shewed them the very psalms which their forefathers had sung as they went up to the Temple and perhaps stopped to rest in this very spot. These are the psalms which are called Songs of Degrees, or Steps, because they were also sung as the pilgrims went up the Temple stair-ways. And the older men joined in with old tales of famous Rabbis, and the girls listened, too, when they had cleared away and packed up.

When it was cool enough to start, they all recited the Evening Prayer and set off. Sometimes a caravan would pass them, going or coming, and the camel-driver and the pilgrims would call out "Shalom," or "Peace be with you!" for it is the Arab salutation also, and sounds much the same in Arabic as in Hebrew. We say "Shalom aleichem," and the Arabs say "Salam aleikum." A party of Arab horsemen was always a little alarming, but it was not very likely the Arabs would venture to attack them lest they should get into trouble with the Russian, the English or some other Consul.

When the mountain-road became steep, the men got down and made the boys ride, which at first they were unwilling to do, wishing to shew off their great strength and endurance before their sisters. But it was a pleasant feeling after the stony road, and it all seemed to them, getting rather drowsy as they jogged along in the moonlight, like a fantastic dream. "Jerusalem, the hills stand round about her," sang the men, and the children began to wonder if the hills would ever end and Jerusalem appear. They were too sleepy to sing themselves. Every now and then they really fell asleep, but the men took good care they should not fall from their seats.

Just as another dawn broke, there was a shout: "Jerusalem!" The boys started wide awake, and all, even the girls, jumped down from the horses and donkeys and cried again and again, "Jerusalem, our dear Jerusalem!"

THE FIRST VIEW OF JERUSALEM

They could not see much of the city from where they were, but they had a feeling that something for which they had longed all their lives, without knowing it, lay now before them. The boys, to whom their master had read bits of Yehuda Halevy's poems, threw themselves upon the ground and kissed it, and, wishing to do as he had done, tied up handfuls of earth in their handkerchief, which they put into their bosoms, because the spot from which the pilgrim first beholds his heart's desire is a holy one to him. The older men, to whom the first sight of Jerusalem was nothing new, wept to see the joy of the children. Morning Prayer was said under the slowly brightening sky, and then the party rode into the town and sought out their friends. These friends were all delighted to see the young boys and girls, and said they would make room for them all in different families.

The first excitement over, the children began to feel very tired, as well they might, and after breakfast they were all made to lie down and fell sound asleep for some hours.

In the evening their master took them out for the first walk about Jerusalem. It would take too long to tell you now all the things they saw and heard during their stay in the holy city—we must leave that for another time.

They spent several days in Jerusalem, enjoyed

themselves immensely, and would have been very sorry when the time came to go home, if they had not been so anxious to tell their parents all they had seen and done. Besides, their new friends all said they must come back next Pentecost, and promised meantime to come and visit them in the Colony, to be entertained and shewn about in their turn. So there was a great deal to look forward to, and they went back very happy.

They also resolved to be very industrious and well-behaved, thus to shew their dear master how sincerely they appreciated his kindness in arranging such a wonderful surprise and treat.

THE FAST

THE FAST

It is two hours before sunset and the whole Colony is in a hurry-scurry. Old and young men are hastening home from the fields, some carrying their scythe, others leading one or two horses, so as to get home in time to wash and make a good meal before the fast, for this evening is Tisha be Av. And in every home the wife is making ready for supper and calling the children together: " Rûn, Dan, and tell your sister to hurry—she is feeding the hens."

" But, mother, I shall have no time to dress ! "

" Dress ! dress ? " exclaimed the mother, " *oi wei !* What are children coming to ? They are losing their Jewish spirit altogether. Is Tisha be Av a holiday ? "

" But I must have my white socks and a clean white Yarmelke, mother, and my slippers—you know I must ! And I hav'n't finished nailing together the little stool for you to sit on."

" Because you left everything to the last minute as usual, and spent the afternoon playing about. Here comes Sarah. Now, children, remember to be very quiet—no tricks and no laughing to-night."

The children sat very quietly through supper, quite sobered by their father's grave face and the mysterious sadness that seemed to fill the little room with the twilight, a great sadness from out the long-ago. Supper ended, parents and children sat down on low stools, a tray with a dish of hard-boiled eggs, some beigels and some ashes were laid on a chair ; each one took an egg, dipped it in the ashes, and ate it together with a beigel. Dan and Sarah knew that the ashes which they used instead of salt were a sign of mourning for the destruction of the second Temple, but it was not so much regret for the Temple that brought the tears into their eyes when their father began to say the blessing as the melancholy tone in which he said it and that strange sadness which seemed to come creeping out of every corner.

After the blessing Dan and his father took their Prayer Books and started for Shool. Then the mother lighted the candles and set out a number of low stools with a chair in the middle, for all her near neighbours would be coming in to pray.

When Sarah had finished helping her mother to put away the supper things and to arrange the room, she went to the window and watched the people pass on their way to the Shool, men and boys and a few elderly women, all carrying their slippers and stools to sit on, because on

Tisha be Av they were not supposed to wear shoes or to sit on any real seat. The stocking-feet made no noise; even the little boys walked along in silence; the only sounds in the Colony came from the animals—the clucking of a neighbour's hens and the bray of his donkey seemed unusually loud to Sarah this evening.

Meantime her brother Dan was standing among his little companions in the Shool, his Prayer Book open, but his eyes fixed on the Chazan, except when he had to wipe them with his sleeve, overcome by the desolate chant and by the sobs of the old women in the gallery. When the prayers were over and the boys out again in the fresh air, they felt brighter, and, while their fathers stood talking together, the children gathered in a rush and began to talk about the Fast and how much of it they meant to keep. Abraham had decided to keep the whole, though he was not yet Bar Mitzvah, and could do as he pleased about it.

"So will I fast," said Dan; "no food and no water for me till to-morrow evening."

"Very silly of you," said Moses. "Who expects a boy of eleven to go without food and drink for twenty-four hours? I, of course, shall fast like Abraham, so as to get into the way of it by the time I am Bar Mitzvah."

Chaim, the dunce, was of the party, and said that he was going to fast the whole time, too;

but, as Chaim was known to be fond of his meals, the others predicted that he would give in at the sight of the little ones' breakfast.

It was settled that after the Fast they should all meet and tell each other how well they had been able to keep it, and then Dan said good-bye to his friends and went home.

Here he found a room-ful of girls and women sitting on the low stools or on the floor and all crying, while his mother sat on the chair and read aloud the Kinoth or Lamentations. Whenever she came to a very terrible passage they all cried out and then the little children, who had come with their mothers, sobbed aloud with fright and with distress at their mothers' grief. No sooner had they been quieted than a fresh passage set the women crying, and every time this happened the small children howled more loudly, so that the whole thing became pandemonium till the Lamentations were ended, when the visitors all got up and took the children home to bed.

"I am so thirsty," whispered Dan to Joseph, who had come in for a few minutes on his way home, and was sitting beside his friend on the floor in a corner; "however shall I be able to hold out all day to-morrow?"

"You won't be so thirsty when you wake," said Joseph, "and besides, what is the good of fasting if you don't suffer? The thirstier you are the more you will suffer and the more acceptable it will be in God's sight."

This made Dan feel pleased with himself, and he wished to be very hungry too, to shew God that he was willing to suffer severely for his religion.

Next day neither the men nor the boys felt inclined to do much, and the boys ran every half-hour to see if the clock-hand had not gone round. To make things worse, it was a very hot day, and about eleven o'clock three or four of the boys became so restless that they decided to go and visit some of their friends and see how they were bearing the Fast.

They found Joseph lying with his face pressed to the cool mosaic floor of his father's house.

"Well, Joseph," said Abraham, "how do you feel?"

"As you see," said Joseph; "it is a hard thing to be a Jew."

"Did you think it was an easy one? The master said that anyone who found it easy was not a real Jew, whoever he might be, and that a Fast is to discipline us, so that we should be ready to bear hardness whenever it came our way. I am all dried up myself."

"Oh dear, oh dear, I wish it were sunset!"

sighed Joseph, laying his face on to a fresh piece of marble.

"Never mind," said Moses, "it will do you good. Father wanted me to have some coffee and a beigel, but I would not—I am quite old enough to pass a day without food. Get up, Joseph, and let us all go and see Dan. The sooner we get out of this place the better, because I can smell the good things your mother is cooking for to-night, and it makes me feel rather bad."

They went to Dan's house, but could not find him. They looked for him indoors and out, and had just concluded he must have gone to Shul with his father, when they heard a sound of weeping inside the barn. It was unmistakably Dan's voice, so they pushed open the door and went in.

There lay Dan on the straw shaken with sobs. It was some time before they could persuade him to sit up and tell them what had happened. Even then he sobbed between his words and seemed ashamed to look them in the face.

"You won't speak to me," he said, "when you know what I did; you will call me coward and despise me."

"Well, but tell us, tell us," cried the others.

Then he told them that he had fasted till past noon, though he felt very hungry and weak, and had kept up his spirits by remembering what Joseph had said to him: "The more you suffer the better in the end." But he could not help lingering about the kitchen sniffing the cakes and the stewed fruits his mother was preparing for supper, and it happened that, just as his mother had taken a tray of delicious cheese-cakes out of the oven, she was called away and he was left alone with them on the table. Before she came back, he had eaten three.

"Oh," exclaimed the others, "what a greedy boy!"

"I don't know what possessed me," sighed Dan; "I simply could not resist the temptation. When mother came back, she missed the cakes and she told me I was a very wicked boy. I was a thief because I had taken the cakes while her back was turned, and I was a dreadful hypocrite for pretending to fast and eating on the sly. I don't so much mind what mother said to me (here came a fresh burst of tears), but I wanted so much to fast and to feel I could control myself, as the master said we should be able to, and now he and you will all look down upon me, and God will not so soon forgive me."

The rest sat quiet for a moment, and then Moses said: "See what comes of being greedy."

"And what are *you*," cried Dan, blazing up all of a sudden. What are *you* to talk about me being greedy? What about that honey and those figs and that melon and . . . ."

"Stop! stop!" said Abraham, "we must not quarrel on a Fast day; let us each forget that the other was greedy, and then we shall not be reproached for having been greedy ourselves. Come, boys, we will go and look for our master and ask him what Dan ought to do now."

Dan did not want to face the master, so the others said they would go for him and ask the teacher's advice without mentioning Dan by name. Dan remained sitting on the straw.

Presently his friends came back and said they were sorry, but the master had gone to Jaffa, so they would have to wait till next day.

"Let us get a Bible," said Joseph, "and see what we can find about repentance, and how a person can make up for breaking a Fast which he had promised to keep."

"The master once read us a bit of Isaiah about fasting," said Dan, brightening up; "I will ask for a Bible and we will try to find it."

He ran indoors and soon came back with a Bible, which he handed to Abraham, who sat down cross-legged on the barn floor, with the book on his knee, and the other boys clustered round. After some turning of pages, the chapter in question was found and read. It proved all that was needed, for it told plainly that fasting is a small thing compared with charity. Dan gave a sigh of relief and said : " I will put all my savings into our box for the poor, and every day for a week I will give away a bit of my dinner to the poor Arab children."

" Now," said Abraham, " you may as well go and eat a little more, seeing that your Fast is broken once for all."

But Dan would not hear of that, and said that fasting till sunset would be a pleasure to him. " And really," he said, " I am even more hungry than I was before I ate those cheese-cakes, and am suffering more than any of you. They have also made me more thirsty."

Moses, who felt sorry for having called Dan greedy, put his arm round his neck and said: " Let us all go and see what Chaim is doing. He was bragging the whole week about keeping the fast, but I am sure he has had two meals at least by now."

They all went to Chaim's house and found him on the sofa with his mother beside him trying to persuade him to have some food.

" Look at this silly boy," she cried to the others as they came in, " he will be ill. What does he want to fast for, when he is not Bar Mitzvah ? Tell him to be sensible and eat."

" Why, Chaim ! " explained the boys, " surely you hav'n't fasted till now ? "

Chaim smiled weakly but proudly, and pushed away the plate his mother was holding. Before the others had recovered from their astonishment, Chaim's mother had left the room and returned with a tumbler of water. Seizing Chaim's head, she managed to pour some of the water into his mouth, so that he was obliged to swallow it. "There," she said to the choking Chaim, "now your fast is broken and you may as well eat."

Chaim shook his head violently, but Abraham said: "See here, Chaim, we know you meant to fast all day and that you would have done it, but, if you continue to resist your mother, you will be breaking the Fifth Commandment and then your fasting will not help you; so eat what she has brought you, and God will accept your fast such as it is."

Chaim was very pleased to hear this, and to think he could eat without losing the good opinion of the other boys. His mother asked them to sit down and refresh themselves also, but they thanked her and left the house in haste, fearful of further temptation. They did not want to be in their own homes either, where their mothers were cooking, filling the air with appetizing smells, so first they lay down and slept an hour or two in a shady place, and then they went into the garden and picked water-melons for the evening."

NEW YEAR'S EVE

NEW YEAR'S EVE

It was a New Year's Eve! The sun was setting in his glory and a wonderful stillness reigned throughout the Colony. People were walking leisurely toward the synagogue—even Abraham and Moses, the most mischievous of the boys, walked in a subdued manner beside their parents, not even thinking of teasing their sisters, for was not this the Eve of the New Year, when all beings came for judgment before the Throne of the God of Israel?

In the synagogue all was light, and everyone was praying earnestly. When service was ended, all lingered outside to wish each other a "Happy New Year," hoping that God might permit them to meet again in health and happiness the following New Year's Eve. When they got home, each member of each family, from the eldest to the youngest, went up to the Father, who put both his hands on their heads and blessed them. The Mother then embraced and blessed them, with tears in her eyes, and both wished them a "Happy New Year," adding their hope that they might all meet in the same way next year, but with more of the Heavenly Spirit in them.

The Father then made kiddush, and the goblet of wine was handed round to each member of the family to taste. Then hands were washed, grace was said, and they began the Feast by dipping bread into the honey, as a sign that they hoped the New Year might start with sweetness. During the Feast, hymns were sung; and, when that was over, all the family went for a walk in the moonlight. The moon was in her full glory and made them feel that she, too, shared the hope of a bright New Year.

The next morning, all the boys were up and in synagogue at 6 o'clock, and said their prayers with special earnestness and attention: when it came to u-nesane-tokef, and when the Shofer blew (that is the trumpet made out of a ram's horn which is blown every New Year's morn), the boys wept bitterly; for they knew they had committed many sins against God and their neighbours, and they began to remember how often they had been really unkind and spiteful to one another, how they had teased their sisters, and also had told tales about each other, and stolen fruit from neighbours' orchards—really more for the fun of it than for the longing for the fruit, for they all had plenty of their own, oranges, figs, nuts, melons, and grapes.

When the Chazan read from the Prayer Book the part where it is written: " If there is true repentance and an earnest wish to avoid the same sins in the future, and alms given to the poor—then God would forgive all past sins," the boys in their inmost hearts repented sincerely, and determined to try hard to turn over a new leaf and be better boys, and they also resolved that they would take all their savings and put them in the charity-boxes which always hang in every home.

They left the synagogue in a very much happier mood, feeling they had performed their first New Year's duty. When walking home, Abraham asked Joseph and Simon what plans they had thought of, for even on that day they felt they must all be together.

Joseph said: " Of course, we must go to Tashlich in the afternoon, and it will take over an hour getting to the river, so we had better spend the morning in repeating Psalms to each other."

Chaim, the dunce, said that he would like to join them.

" No! no!" the others all shouted; " we don't want to lag behind our parents!"

At this Chaim started crying, and said: " Oh, you horrid boys!—even on New Year's Day you are unkind!"

The boys looked at one another and felt guilty, for they knew that what Chaim had said was true, and that no sooner had they left the synagogue than they had forgotten their good resolutions. So they dropped their heads in shame and quietly said : "All right, Chaim ! You can come along with us ; but you must try to walk faster."

So it was settled that, after the mid-day meal, and their families had had a rest, the boys would walk together to the river, each carrying his Psalm Book.

They saw their teacher, when they arrived there, and, after wishing him a "Happy New Year," they stood near him, repeating the special Psalms for Tashlich.

While they were deep in their devotions they heard a splash—and then piercing shrieks. For a moment no one knew what had happened, till Chaim's head appeared in the water,a nd he made a great ado, splashing and shouting. Everyone rushed to see what had happened ; but, before others thought of doing anything to help, Moses jumped in, caught hold of Chaim, and swam with him to the river-bank.

The ever-ready hands of the teacher dragged the two out of the water. He helped them undress themselves, and laid their clothes out on the sand to dry.

THEY HEARD A LOUD SPLASH AND THEN PIERCING SHRIEKS

While the clothes were drying and Chaim stood naked, the people gathered round him and asked how he managed to fall in.

Chaim said : " Dan pushed me in."

" It's a lie ! " said Dan ; " I never pushed him in. He may have slipped in, *unknowingly*, for Chaim was imitating the Chassidim, bending and shaking backwards and forwards, when saying his prayers, and he must have forgotten that he was so near the steep bank of the river, and, when bending a little too far forward must have slipped."

" No ! no ! " again cried Chaim ; " Dan pushed me in," and, whimpering, added : " No one ever believes me ; for the boys always make me out a liar, because they do not like me."

Abraham had a very kind heart and did not want the joy of the New Year to be spoilt by any ill-feeling, so he said : " Hear me, boys ! *I* know who did it ! Oh ! how I wish it had been done to me ! "

" Who ? who ? " all exclaimed. " Tell us ! tell us ! " they shouted.

His teacher, hearing what Abraham had said, came nearer and smilingly said : " Tell us, thou wise son of Israel ! "

" Why ! of course it was Chaim's good Angel that did it ! " said Abraham. " Chaim is always doing wrong, he says, *without knowing !* His

Angel knew we often call him a dullard, and we blame and pay him out for the wrong he does, even though he does do it in ignorance. So when Chaim came to be judged for his last year's sins, his good Angel pitied him and asked God to deal with him mercifully. For is it not written in Isaiah i.: 'Wash you, make you clean . . . though your sins be as scarlet, they shall be as white as snow.' Well, the Angel knew that Chaim was—like the hypocrite—not thinking as much about the prayers he was saying as of copying the Chassidim, so he pushed him into the river; and, as he had on his scarlet tunic, you see he went in as scarlet as his sins, and now he is white like snow! And this proves that all his sins have been forgiven him!"

While Abraham was speaking, Chaim began to feel quite pleased, for he felt he was really becoming a hero. Nothing else could have given him so much pleasure, for all his life long he had been snubbed for one thing or another and constantly called a dunce or a dullard. Even the boys who heard Abraham's idea believed for a minute that Chaim had been rewarded for never *intentionally* doing wrong, and that his had been a special sign of God's favour.

The next minute, however, they saw a twinkle in Abraham's eyes, for he had seen his teacher smiling at him as if he knew his intention of wanting to be kind to Chaim on New Year's Day. Then they all understood, and a giggle went round, and then there was a silence for a time. Then the teacher took advantage of it and said: "Come, boys, and you girls, too, let us sit nearer the river and have a little talk about this day and the religious customs connected with it, for you know they have an inner spiritual meaning."

They always enjoyed his talks, so gladly gathered near him.

"You all know," he continued, "that this is a season of peculiar solemnity, for God, knowing our mortal and evil inclinations, in time long past, gave us in His great mercy certain days in every year in which to carefully examine our past thoughts or intentions as well as our past words or deeds. So the Shofar sounded this morning a it has sounded every year, and bade us awake from our spiritual apathy and indifference. What does the old year say when bidding you loving farewell? 'Boyhood is the age for fun and frolic, but laugh and be merry at proper times and seasons.' If you work earnestly when you are at work, you will play more earnestly when playing. Human life is given to us for the development of our immortal souls. They are tested and trained through sorrow, suffering, and disappointment, and sometimes through riches. Let us not be found wanting! You know, of course, that the Shofar is blown at this season to commemorate our Father Abraham's intended sacrifice of his well-beloved son Isaac on Mount Moriah. Of all the tests that Father Abraham had from God, this one was the greatest proof of his devotion and obedience ; for God had promised him and Sarah that ' in Isaac all nations of the world would be blessed ' ; so we, too, must endeavour to be as devoted and obedient as our Father Abraham wa . God has promised never to try us more than we are able to bear, but will with the trial make a way of escape as he did for Abraham, when He saw that Abraham had prepared everything needed for the sacrifice in obedience to His command. He had another offering ready (the ram caught in the thicket) for Abraham to offer as a sacrifice. In the coming ten Penitential Days always remember that all our outward signs of repentance will be of no avail in God's sight, unless we prove our inward regret by acknowledging our sins to God and asking those we have wronged or injured in word or in deed or in thought to forgive us, and also do our utmost to right the wrong or repay the injury, for then only can our sins be forgiven us by God."

The boys were all very silent and serious after their master's discourse, for they knew how true his words were. Dan who was sitting next to him, said : " Master, I confess openly that it was through my fault that Chaim fell into the river. I did not do it purposely, but, as I was pushing some pebbles into the water with my foot, I nearly slipped and tried to catch hold of Chaim to steady myself, as he was shaking like Chassidim when saying his prayers, he fell forwards. When I touched him, he lost his balance, and somehow or other I did not, and so he fell in."

"Well, I am pleased to hear you, my boy," said the master, and gave him a hearty shake of the hand. "I know how hard it is to confess openly our misdoings or sins; for, while we are confessing them, we feel how wicked or mean we have been, and this feeling of shame helps to prevent our doing the same thing again. This is why in some cases our Rabbis advise a Public Confession. Now that you have confessed how it all happened, let us hope that in future you will try to be more careful, for much pain and damage is often done to man and beast through carelessness or thoughtlessness. We all like to see boys and girls have their play and fun; but while taking it let them be careful not to hurt others either by word or by deed. God has given us a beautiful world, therefore let us enjoy it without, if possible, injuring it."

The rest of the boys went up to shake hands with the master, and said that they would do what he asked and try to seriously think over their past conduct and try to do better in the future. The only one who was not pleased with the turn things had taken was Chaim, for he was no longer a hero in the sight of the others.

Even they did not walk home as merrily as they had come out—for each in his inmost heart knew that he had some hard tasks before him yet before his sins could be forgiven on the Day of Atonement.

Our next chapter will tell how each tried to amend his failings of the past year.

THE DAY OF ATONEMENT

THE DAY OF ATONEMENT

During the ten Penitential Days before the Day of Atonement there was no need as usual for the fathers to call the boys, as all got up at dawn. They went willingly to the synagogue, for which, as a rule, they did not much care; but now, after their teacher's talk on New Year's Day, it was their own wish to make as much atonement for their sins as possible, for the time was so short.

These ten days were very pleasant for the older people, for not only were the boys not mischievous, but they were obedient to everyone. Even to their sisters they behaved nicely and did not tease.

At last the eve of the last day before Atonement Day came. All in the Colony were busy, hurrying and scurrying everywhere, for preparation for feasting was being made in every home. Dainty, tempting things were seen everywhere; yet the boys never touched them, although it was great temptation to them to do so. They felt the All-seeing Eye was watching them.

Now at that time in Palestine it was the custom for a woman or a girl to take a hen, and a man or a boy a cock, to hold them by their feet and swing the birds round above their heads, while a prayer was addressed to God that He would accept the bird as a sacrifice as of old, before the Temple was burnt. Then the bird was killed for the Feast, and some of it was given to the poor. If a family was well-to-do, every child or member of the household had a hen or a cock for a sacrifice; if poor, a bird was divided. Then the birds were killed and roasted for the Feast. Everyone tried to have a white bird for the sacrifice, and for months before the Day of Atonement the children in the Colony used to try and rear white cocks and hens. In those days there were not many white ones in Judea, and so they had to do with whatever they could get.

Now both Joseph's and Moses' sisters had all white hens, but they had no white cocks. This made the brothers wild, so, when their sisters asked them to help them catch the hens in the farm-yard, they thought that this was a lovely chance to tease them. Every time their sisters nearly caught a hen, in some way or other the boys interfered, and the bird managed to escape. This went on for some time and the girls got both hot and tired. Then they watched more closely and found that instead of helping them, the boys did the opposite. So they scolded them well and told them they were very unkind, and that even on the Eve of Yom Kippur they did not try to be good.

The boys felt very uncomfortable for they knew they had transgressed again. So they left the girls and went to help their mothers milk the cows, carry the water from the well, and sweep and clean the farm-yard and porch, in this way hoping to make amends for their transgression. Their mothers were surprised at their good behaviour and thought they had really turned over a new leaf with the New Year—which they really wanted to do, but there always seemed some temptation in the way!

Next day, when after mid-day all came from the fields, there was indeed plenty to do and very little time to do it in—first to get things straight for the meal before the Fast of Yom Kippur, and then to provide the next day's food for the cattle (for although they fasted themselves the cattle must have their food), and they could not work on the morrow, as it was a Holy Day.

In a few hours, however, all was finished and the place quiet again. Men, women, and even children were all dressed in white, as it had always been the custom so to dress on that day, and a beautiful custom it is, for white is the symbol of purity, for which our religion stands. In ancient days, on Yom Kippur even the High Priest wore white garments. This custom expresses the Hebrew thought that the men and women of our nation are priests and priestesses of our religion, by the example of their life in the sacred sanctuary as well as in the home and daily place of business or work; for by worship, home-life, and labour for our children, the future men and women of Israel are best trained to loyalty to God and to human ideals.

They all went to Mincha (the afternoon service in the synagogue), and when they returned home they all sat down to have their last meal before sunset. Till after sunset next day not a drop of water or food would pass their lips, although the Law allowed young children to eat and drink until they were thirteen years old. Many of the children in our Colony, from nine years of age would insist on fasting, and were happy in feeling that they too could keep this Law.

Then the Mother, the "Priestess of the Home," lighted the Sabbath lamps for Yom Kippur called in the Bible the "Sabbath of Sabbaths,' so holy and solemn a day was it ordained to be; and they all were blessed by their Fathers and Mothers, and forgiveness was asked of them for all they had done that had been wrong.

After sunset, the stillness, would have made even a stranger think that all the inhabitants had left the village, except that from a distance was heard a sad, beautiful melody (the Kol Nidre) sung by the Chazan, and from time to time were heard men and women joining in with cries and sobs. The boys in the synagogue were praying with deep emotion and awe, for were they not all standing before the Creator and Judge of all mankind, and how could they expect to be forgiven for all the wrong things they had done during the past year? Then the Chazan read from that part of the Prayer Book that God will not forgive us until we have forgiven those who have wronged us, nor until we have asked those we had wronged to forgive us, and striven our best to make good to the people whom we had hurt or wronged. Those words made them extra sorrowful, for it was such an unpleasant thing to think of going to and confessing to the people they had wronged and to ask forgiveness of them. In fact, when the Chazan read out: "For the sins which we have committed before Thee under compulsion or of our own free will," they beat their breasts extra hard.

At last the service was over, and when the people met outside the synagogue those who had quarrelled during the past year made friends with each other, asking forgiveness, each one realizing that there are nearly always faults on both sides in every quarrel.

Most of the boys walked together, and then sat down on some hay near Abraham's home. They all shook hands, and asked each other to forgive any unkind thing they had done during the past year. Even Chaim was treated with kindness and gentleness.

After a while Joseph said: "My conscience feels very guilty, for I made up my mind on New Year's Day, after our master's talk on the river-bank, that I would go to Reb Shmuel and tell him it was I who let all the horses and oxen out of his barn that Saturday, and you know what a lot of damage they did, when they got into the wheat-field, for not only did they eat a good deal of corn, but they spoiled a lot more by trampling on it. I did it to pay him out for pulling my ears, when I stayed out of synagogue while prayers were going on. I am sure he would never forgive me if he knew it was I who did it, for he thinks it was Abdul the young Arab."

Dan said he, too, had done wrong, for one Saturday he went to Jeremiah's bee-hives, and let the bees all out, and then took a lot of honey, ate some, and the rest he hid for eating later on. That was not all, for the bees got very savage at being disturbed, and stung all who passed by;

even some little children had their faces bitten and swollen.

"Oh I remember! I remember," they all shouted, "for there were about a dozen people going about with swollen lips and cheeks or hands"—and they all laughed at the recollection of the funny sight they had been, and they also remembered how angry Jeremiah had been, and how he had tried to find the culprit and had said that if he *did* find him he would whip him in the open street near the Well so that all should know.

"It is indeed serious," they said to one another; "but what could they do?"—for both Joseph and Dan stood between God and the people they had harmed or injured. If they would not confess and ask Reb Shmuel and Jeremiah to forgive them, God would not forgive them, and yet if they confessed they knew they would be punished. That, they would not mind, but what was far worse was they were ashamed that all in the Colony would know that they had done it and had been so long in confessing it.

Their hearts were failing them when Dan said: "You remember, boys, on New Year's Day I confessed what I did when Chaim fell into the river, and, believe me, I felt as ashamed as you do now; but after I had openly confessed, I felt very much happier, and I really think I would have gone through much more to feel as happy as I did. It was like taking a plunge into the sea—at first you feel cold and shivery; then you begin to feel a lovely warm glow all over you."

"I dare not, I dare not," said Joseph and Moses; "*yours* was only an accident; you didn't *mean* to push him in, but ours are very great sins, for they caused the Reb Shmuel and Jeremiah a loss of money, and the people bitten great pain."

Abraham, who always had a bright idea ready (especially in times of difficulty) started up, and said: "Come, let us tell our master; he is a good man and will show us the best way to do it."

So they went to the master's house, and told him their trouble. He, too, felt it was a very serious matter, but he insisted that the only right thing to do was to go to the injured people and make a brave open confession. Feeling how very hard it would be for the boys to do this, he kindly offered to go with them.

It was no easy time. The injured ones, when they heard who had done the deed, felt very, very angry and were inclined to give the boys a good sound thrashing. The master, however, reminded them that it was Yom Kippur night, and perhaps they, too, might have done something, *knowingly* or *unknowingly*, that was wrong, and also needed God's forgiveness, and they could not expect it if they would not forgive the boys. So, after this good piece of advice which the teacher gently gave them, they forgave the lads and sent them home.

Although the boys fasted all the next day, they felt bright and happy, for in their inmost hearts they knew that God was pleased for doing what He had commanded.

THE FEAST OF TABERNACLES:

OR

THE MAKING OF THE SUCCAH

THE FEAST OF TABERNACLES, OR THE MAKING OF THE SUCCAH

THERE were only two more days before the Festival began, and yet no sign of a booth was to be seen anywhere about the homes of Abraham, Joseph, and Moses. In every other home the skeletons of the booths were up and they needed only the final decoration. (In Palestine the rules for making the Succah were very strictly carried out, and every household had a booth erected in which, if there was room, the men, women, and children, spent seven days), as at that season of the year it was nice and warm. The men used to sleep in them, so as to carry out the words of the Bible : " Ye shall dwell in booths seven days, so that your generations may know that I made the children of Israel to dwell in booths, when I brought thcm out of the Land of Egypt. I am the Lord your God "—Leviticus xxiii. This festival is also called the " Feast of Ingathering," as it was commanded through Moses that they should present themselves in the Sanctuary of the Lord with their offerings : " Thou shalt observe the Feast of Tabernacles seven days, after that thou hast gathered in thy corn and thy wine (which is at the close of the year), and thou shalt rejoice in thy Feast, thou and thy children and thy men and maidservants, and the Levite and stranger, and the fatherless and widows that are within thy gates"—Exodus xxiii., Deuteronomy xvi.

Now let us go back to our three friends. Their mother came out and scolded the boys for not having their booth ready, as everyone else had; but they told her not to worry, as they would have it all ready in good time. This year these friends, who were inseparable, had decided to make their booths so beautiful that there would not be another equal to them; and this could be done only if they left it to the very last, for generally all were so keen to have theirs look the best that often, if they saw one they liked better, they would undo theirs and copy it. So, to prevent having to do this, the three boys had left theirs till the very last. They also wanted to surprise their parents, but this was difficult, for they had no patience, and started erecting the booth themselves. Seeing this, Joseph said to Abraham: "It is not wise trying to keep the secret; let us take our Mothers into our confidence and they will manage in some way to satisfy our Fathers."

So they told their Mothers their plan, and they smiled and promised to keep their Fathers quiet, for they knew what a pleasure it would be to the boys to do everything without help, and it only happened once a year. They told them, however, that they must let their sisters know, as it would take them some time to weave the garlands of flowers and to plait the wheat and make beautiful ornaments from God's beautiful earth.

Although the boys were not keen to have their sisters know, yet they realized that they could not very well do without them, as they were so handy in these matters. " It is a real nuisance," said Moses, " to think we can never do anything without those girls ! Whatever is started among ourselves we have to bring them in ! "

" Ah well ! " said Abraham, " you see that is why God had to give Eve to Adam, for even the first man couldn't manage by himself, although he had very little to do at that time—just to take care of the Garden of Eden. So when God saw this He gave Eve to be Adam's helpmate. You had better not let the girls hear your opinion of them, Moses, for, after all, they can be very useful, and sometimes, too, have very good ideas of their own."

" Oh, well, well ! " said Moses, " I suppose you're right, but all the same I'd sooner we did without them if we could."

The next evening the boys started work by moonlight, stealing quietly out of the Colony, to meet their young Arab friend Abdul, who was waiting for them.

That young Arab simply worshipped those Jewish boys, and felt greatly honoured when they allowed him to help them in their pranks. Now he waited for them with a large sack, saw, and hatchet, to help the boys to cut branches off the trees and vines to decorate the booths. This went on for two nights, and then on the last day before the Festival each boy started carrying his bundle of decorations home.

Suddenly Abraham exclaimed: "I thought each of us was to have his different from the others; but they will be much the same."

They dropped their bundles and stood staring at each other and rubbing their heads.

Suddenly the young Arab said: "Near our village are some palm-trees, and I can easily climb up and break off some branches."

"Good! good!" they all shouted, and slapped him on the shoulder; "why, you are quite clever, Abdul!"

The Arab felt he had received the highest praise that could be given, and a broad grin spread over his face. So they left their bundles and followed Abdul.

When they got close to the Arab village all the dogs started barking, and they feared all the village would awake and attack them, for they had not forgotten their adventure with the shepherd-boys on last Chanuka ; but Abdul said that it would be all right. The dogs would soon stop, and the Arabs seldom took any notice of the barking.

Abdul then climbed up one of the palm trees as quickly as a monkey, picked off some of the branches, and threw them down to the boys. When they had enough, they tied them with ropes into large bundles and returned to where they had left the others.

Then Joseph exclaimed: " Even now, we sha'n't each have a different booth ! "

Here was a puzzle—what could they do ?

" Never mind," said Moses ; " I'll give in this time, for we are tired and still have a lot to do. You, Abraham, have the palms, and you, Joseph, the branches of cedar and olive trees, and I will have part of each and a few willows. So each booth will be different."

Then then hurried home, much to Abdul's disappointment, for he started crying when they said they could not let him help in making the Succah, as it was the Law that Israelites alone were to do it.

Then he begged to be allowed to hand them the branches whilst they were decorating the booths, and do other little things to help, and to this they agreed.

Then all three boys started first to build Abraham's booth, for they always looked on him as their leader. They dug the holes to put the posts in, and, when the frame work was finished, they began entwining the boughs and vine-branches and lightly covering the top with them, too, so that the sun could be seen through the branches during the day and the moon during the night, as it is written.

When all this was done Abraham went into the house and brought out some white sheets and dark-coloured curtains to throw over the booth, so that the other boys and girls could not see inside till all was finished. Then each helped to build Joseph's and Moses' booths, only instead of cedar and olive branches theirs were decorated with palms and willow branches; and by the time all this was finished the cocks began to crow.

They then decided to take a little rest, for there was yet much to do. After a short rest, they went to the river and got some myrtle and thinner branches of willow to plait into rings so as to hold the lulav, and also for the garlands of flowers and wheat. Then they went into the orange-grove and picked the finest oranges.

Meanwhile, the girls and young women were decorating the Succah by hanging the garlands of flowers along the walls. Oranges also were hung from the roof of the booths, tied to the twigs with gaily-coloured ribbons; also pomegranates, lemons, figs, almonds, and bunches of black and of white grapes and other kinds of fruit.

Then they hung up ribbons, and little bottles of olive-oil and wine of different kinds. Between the garlands of flowers hung pictures of the Patriarchs Abraham and Moses and other great men. Then near the wall facing the door (for each booth had a door) stood a table, and on it was placed a large basket decorated with natural ornaments, such as barley, wheat, and various-coloured leaves twined round it. In the middle of the basket was placed a large melon with other fruits. In one corner of the booth was another small table or stand covered with a white cloth, and on it was placed an ornamental jar filled with water, and in it was the lulav, and a glass vase or silver jar in which was placed the citron (one that was carefully picked to be without blemish) bedded in wadding. Oh, how carefully the citron was handled!—for no one was allowed to touch it with a finger till it had been taken to the synagogue and prayers said over it, and it had been shaken. Then the citron was handed to the Mother, and then to the rest of the family, the oldest coming first. It was even put into the hands of babies, but, of course, the Father or the Mother held it so that the little ones should not drop it and let it get bruised, for no blemish must be on the offerings that we bring to God—all must be of the very best.

When they opened the Succah door and saw how beautifully the girls had decorated it, they just stood and gasped for breath; for it was a sight to see! Even Moses was satisfied, and said: "It's really a blessing to have some of the girls to help, for they have taste."

The sun was sinking towards the west and it was time for everyone to get ready to go to the synagogue. So they hurried indoors, and in a short time all came out ready. Before going to synagogue, they had a last peep to see if all was right in the Succah. In the meantime, their Mother had put chairs round the table and placed two silver candlesticks with lighted candle on the table, and two loaves were covered with white silk—embroidered covers that are used only on Holy Days. Also, she had put the bottle of wine with the glass ready for making Kiddush after they had returned from synagogue.

When Abraham saw it all, he felt that all the hard work he had done during the last two nights and days was nothing to the joy he felt when he looked at the Succah finished, and realized what a blessing it was to be a true Israelite, and to live in a land where they were able to obey the ancient Law. Doing so brought such joy, light, and brightness into their lives, for did not King David truly say: "Thy Law is a lamp unto my feet, and a light unto my path." Yes, indeed, all the sufferings of the Jews for so many generations past are nothing compared to the joy they feel in following the Law.

He then went with the rest of the family to synagogue, and, when returning home, it was like fairy-land to see all the lights shining through the many Succahs, built all over the Colony, and there was joy in every home in Palestine that night.

SIMCHAS TORAH:

OR

'REJOICING IN THE LAW'

SIMCHAS TORAH OR "REJOICING IN THE LAW."

DURING the week of Tabernacles the boys and girls had a grand time. They went out pic-nicing and visiting different Arab villages, and the boys were gladly lent horses to ride, while the girls were lent donkeys, as they were not such good riders as their brothers.

The Arab children, and even the men and women, looked forward to the coming of the Judean children, as they called them; for they used to bring them presents of cakes and other dainties that they never had a chance of tasting at any other time. Arabs are more greedy than Europeans, for they get so little.

Now on the last day of Tabernacles, when they could not ride after the mid-day meal, the boys went for a long walk, and on returning some went into the orange-grove and some into the hut in the vineyard. As they were very hot and tired they fell fast asleep, and only awoke when the sun was setting.

On suddenly awakening the boys in the orange-grove halloed to the boys in the vineyard, and all started racing to the synagogue ; for it was the eve of Simchas Torah, and during the service all the scrolls of the Law, large and small, are covered with specially beautiful silks and silver bells.

Each member is called up by the warden and given one of the scrolls to carry in the procession round the synagogue, while psalms and hymns of praise and thanksgiving are being chanted.

With great joy the boys always looked forward to this Simchas Torah service, because of the honour of carrying one of the scrolls, the smaller ones being given to the younger boys. Even the tiny tots carried coloured flags with the words : " Rejoicing in the Law," painted on them. An apple dipped in toffee was stuck on top of the flag-stick.

After the procession was over, bags of sweets, and fruit, and cakes were given to the children.

The synagogue, too, looked extra bright with the specially lighted candles and the many-coloured clothes of the congregation. Even babies were dressed in bright colours for that occasion.

So you can imagine with what excitement the boys ran to the synagogue fearing all the time they might be too late ; but they managed to arrive just after the Evening Prayer, as the procession was forming and the scrolls were being taken out of the Ark; and it was with a great sigh of relief that they slipped into their places without being noticed.

That night in every home there was feasting and singing. Anyone who was too poor to have a feast in his own home was invited by a richer neighbour to come and share his. If anyone felt too proud to accept the invitation, he was even forced to come, for he was told that it was not a private feast, but a public rejoicing, that God had given them the Law, and for that year all the Pentateuch had been read, and next Sabbath they would start again at the beginning.

During the next day's service two men were called up out of the congregation, both called the "Bridegrooms of the Law." One bridegroom closes the reading of the Pentateuch, and the other on the following Sabbath starts the Bible-reading for the New Year with the 1st chapter of Genesis.

What a day of rejoicing it was in the home of the man who closed the year's reading of the Pentateuch, for to be chosen is also considered a great honour.

As the colony at that time only had one synagogue everyone came to partake of the feast prepared in his home. On that day many after the feast walked home unsteadily, and even old grey haired men with long patriarchal beards seemed more lively, and even were sometimes seen dancing. In fact both young and old danced and sang and as there was no music many clapped hands to keep time for the dancers; for it was Simchas Torah and all rejoiced.

Joseph, Dan, Moses, and Simon were not only lively, but drunk or tipsy and did all sorts of queer things. When they wanted more wine their mothers scolded them and said they were making beasts of themselves; but their fathers laughed and said:—"Oh let them have it; for Simchas Torah is only once a year and a little drunkenness is permissable on that day." The boys got so dazed that their sisters or parents had to lead or carry them home to bed, and for the next few weeks they had a very unpleasant time; for their sisters were always reminding them how foolish they looked and acted, and this made them feel that they would take good care not to take too much wine again.

THE CHANUKA

THE CHANUKA

It was drizzling outside on a December evening, with a cutting cold wind; but inside our friend Joseph's house all was excitement and brightness, for it was the first evening of the Feast of Chanuka.

The family all stood round watching their father light the Menorah (the seven-branch oil-lamp, each branch having a little basin of oil and a wick of cotton string through a little float).

As it was the first night only *one* light on the branch was lighted, but this made no difference to the brightness of the room, as there were other lights about. With eager attention Joseph with his brothers and sisters listened and joined in the prayers and song while the wick was being lighted.

When this was done neighbours and friends dropped in, for it was winter and there was very little outside work to be done, and during the Festival week it is the general custom of those who can afford it to invite their friends and neighbours—in fact whoever came was welcomed.

Shortly afterwards Joseph's mother had the pancakes and tea handed round to the guests. Pancakes or dough-nuts are always prepared for the Chanuka Festival. After they had finished eating the pancakes, the boys and girls begged their old Rabbi to tell them some of the Bible stories of those days, for, though they heard them every year, they were never tired of listening to them.

He told them that after Alexander the Great, of Macedon, who conquered King Darius of Persia, died, his kingdom was divided between four of his generals and they multiplied evil. Antiochus ruled over Syria, and he was succeeded by his son Antiochus Epiphanes. In his reign transgressors of the Law were in Israel, and persuaded many to make a covenant with the nations round about. To this many agreed, and they forsook the Holy Covenant and worshipped the gods of these other nations.

He told them also about the revolt that broke out in Jerusalem among the Jews, headed by Mattathias and his sons; for Antiochus Epiphanes wanted to exterminate the Jewish Religion and to force the Greek Religion on the Jews. As the greater part of the Jews would nor worship idols, he marched against them, and put 40,000 of them to death in three days, and sold as many for slaves.

THE FAMILY ALL STOOD ROUND WATCHING THE FATHER LIGHTING MENORAH

Then the Rabbi told them how Epiphanes entered the Temple, stripped it of its treasures, and put up a statue to Jupiter Olympus, and commanded, under penalty of torture to death, all to bow down and worship this god. When the misery of the Jews who would not do this became well nigh unbearable, Mattathias and his five sons came forward and marched against the Syrians and the Greeks, who fled, and the Jews returned victorious. The first thing Mattathias and his followers did was to cleanse and repair the Temple; and, while doing this, they found a small cruse of oil that had been hidden out of sight of the idolaters, and with it they were able to light the sacred lamps. Though there was very little oil in the cruse, yet it fed the lamps for the week; and in commemoration of this wonderful delivery the Menorah is lighted yearly during this Festival both in the synagogues and in our homes.

"As you know my children," said the old Rabbi, "the festival is kept as a memorial of God's mercy in rescuing His people"—then the Rabbi stopped and bowed his head in thought, forgetting the people around him, and seeming to be thinking only of those bygone days.

While he sat there musing, the children felt that Mattathias, the brave leader of old, must have looked like their old stately Rabbi, with his long Patriarchal white head as he sat, deep in thought. Suddenly the door opened, and he awoke as if from a dream and said: "My friends and children, I am an old man; my days on earth are numbered, and I cannot expect to live to see our land our own again, but I earnestly believe that God in His mercy may yet allow our people to possess it once again, and live once again peacefully amongst their own vineyards and fig-trees; but I pray earnestly that it may come about, not by the sword but by the spirit or work of God. For did He not say by the prophet Zechariah: 'Not by might nor by power but by My Spirit?'"

As he finished they all earnestly said Amen, and there was perfect silence for a few minutes, as if each was inwardly offering up a prayer.

Then the hostess and girls brought in supper, and young and old were invited to partake of it.

When supper was over and grace had been said, one of the girls said: "Rabbi, did not women take any share in this delivering of our people?"

"Yes, yes," exclaimed the Rabbi, "there were indeed some noble and brave women, but it is too late to-night to tell about them. To-morrow we are invited to Reb Zorach, and when there I will tell you the tale of one noble woman. She was even braver than the men, for she showed the greatness of her love for God in the way she encouraged her seven sons, who were dearer to her than her own life, to be faithful to Him even unto death by torture, for we die but once and personal martyrdom must be easier to bear than the trial of seeing as she saw—seven sons whom she loved more than her life itself, tortured and killed, and yet she never gave way, but continued to encourage them one by one to be faithful to their God. This is one of the greatest things in history."

The girls were delighted that they were going to hear something great of their own sex; so next evening seemed a long time coming. At last as many boys and girls as could squeeze themselves in arrived at Reb Zorach's house, for also those girls who had not been present the night before decided not to miss the treat of hearing the story of this brave woman. Many had to sit on the floor, as the Arabs do, since there were not enough seats for everybody; but it was all the same to the girls, for all they wanted to hear was the story told by the Rabbi.

The hostess, too, was glad to see the large numbers, for she had plenty of willing hands to help her in preparing that night's supper. When the pancakes had as usual been handed round and eaten, they all settled themselves round the Rabbi to listen to his promised tale, and he began : " In the reign of Antiochus Epiphanes there was a Jewish woman who had seven sons. All were God-fearing lads, and their religion was dearer to them, as we shall see, than life itself. They refused to obey Antiochus' command to eat swine's-flesh, and they said they were ready to die rather than transgress the Laws of God. The king, hearing this, became very angry and commanded that each son in turn should be tortured till he agreed to eat swine's-flesh, and if he would not he was to be killed.

" One of the sons when dying said : ' Thou like a fury takest us out of this present life but our God will raise us up unto everlasting life, we who have died sooner than disobey His Law.'

" Another son when dying said : ' It is good being put to death by men to look for hope from God, to be raised up again by Him ; as for thee, O King Antiochus, thou shalt have no resurrection to life.' Antiochus hearing this, got very angry and commanded that they one after another should first be tortured and then put to death.

" At last, after all but one had been tortured and killed, the King had the youngest brought to him and said : ' Look how your brothers have been tortured to death, and you, so young, will you not just put the swine's-flesh to your lips and I will not only spare your life, but I will make you a rich and happy man, and also make you my friend and trust you with my affairs.' The young lad looked the King straight in the face and said: 'Shall I obey an earthly King and disobey the commandments of my Heavenly King, who is The King over Kings? No, rather a thousand deaths than disobey the laws of my Heavenly Father.' Antiochus, hearing these words, admired his courage and had an even greater desire to save him. So he called the lad's mother, and bade her counsel her son to save his life; but she laughed the cruel tyrant to scorn, and said to her son in Hebrew tongue: 'My beloved son, fear not, but go to thy death joyfully and proudly, for God has found you worthy to die in love and obedience to Him, and thy example will give others courage to sacrifice themselves for God and His Laws. Therefore go happily, my son, to death,' and she kissed him and said: 'Put thy whole trust in the Lord.' When she saw him killed, she cried out: 'Blessed be God's Name for ever and ever, and His Will be done,' and she too, fell down dead."

When the Rabbi finished by saying as long as there are such women in Israel we need have no fear that our religion or our nation will ever die out, the women and the girls sobbed bitterly, and even the men and boys wiped tears away from their eyes—and so the evening ended.

Next evening after lighting the Menorah the boys went round to pay visits to their relations and friends, by whom they were given nice things to eat and coins. Some gave coppers, and some gave silver, for it is the custom at this Festival to give the children a present of money or of other things that children like.

So day after day and evening after evening passed very pleasantly. The day before the close of the Festival days Moses and Dan went to a group of boys and said: " Boys, you know Chanuka is nearly over and we've not had any fun! "

" What can we do? "

" Well," said Simon, rubbing his head, " why let's play Judas Maccabeus! "—and the others said: " But how? We ought to have thought of this a week ago, for we have nothing prepared."

" Well, yes, it's rather late," said Moses, " but I'll tell you what; let's just have a little fun and next year we'll prepare earlier."

" What shall we do? " they all shouted. " You know," said Moses, " that outside the Colony near the Arab village there are some boys looking after sheep. Let us dress ourselves up differently; each take a stick, and we'll attack them, but not hurt them, of course. I mean, just give them a little fright." "What," said Moses, "if they attack us, and then if some of the Arabs came out to help them we might be killed." "Nonsense," said Dan, "let's have a fight even if we do get hurt a little; we shall better understand how Judas Maccabeus and his brothers fought, and if we hurt the Arab boys we will tell them that we didn't mean to—it was only a game; and the next day we'll bring them some of our cakes, and you know they would do anything for cakes; and besides they, too, enjoy a game, but of course we will do our best not to hurt them."

So they began to prepare. Next day they had a half-holiday, and after leaving Cheder they met outside the Colony armed with sticks and tin cans to make a noise with. When all were ready they made a sudden rush into the flock of sheep and started to attack the Arab boys.

No sooner did the little Arabs see them than they started shouting, left the sheep, and ran as if for their lives, Moses and the boys flying after them for a short distance.

They then returned home very happy, feeling that they had gained a victory, and decided that next Chanuka they would prepare and make a better attack on an Arab village just to see if they could be heroes like the Maccabees.

So ended Chanuka, only the girls were not pleased that they had not thought of some game too ; but they felt comforted with thinking that they would have their fun, too, next Chanuka.

THE FESTIVAL

THE FESTIVAL

At last Purim was at hand, winter over, the beautiful spring-time ahead. Once more the boys looked forward to their games in the fields of an evening. Besides, Purim itself was a time of great enjoyment, when they could give way to their love of pranks and fun without fear of a scolding. Every Jewish child has a right to be in mischief at Purim, always provided he did no real damage and hurt no one—not that our boys would have done either on purpose.

There were great discussions among them as to how they should celebrate this particular Purim. There would be the usual fun with the rattles in Shool, the usual masquerading, and presents, and they meant to eat as many good things as were to be had, but they wanted to do something extra—they had done so much that was new since they had the master and went to school. Finally they decided to act a play for the grown-ups, and appealed to the master to help them by allotting the characters. This he was very pleased to do, for he appreciated every sign of confidence on his pupil's part; and there was great excitement over the rehearsals and the dressing-up, the girls also having a share in the play. Needless to say, it was taken from the story of Esther.

The Fast of Esther arrived, but none of the children kept it, but spent the day very enjoyably running errands for Mother, pounding sugar and almonds, picking raisins and sesame-seeds for the cakes, bringing in wood and straw for the oven. And when the little cakes were baked and the hot tin laid on the table, the children hung round lovingly, ready to pop a cake into their mouths the instant mother or big sister turned their backs. They often burnt their fingers and tongues—but it was all joy and fun.

As evening drew near, all work was put aside, and old and young dressed themselves in their best. Every house presented a festive appearance. Even in the home of the poorest labourer, and of those Colonists who had but lately arrived from Russia, and were still full of care and trouble, gloom gave way to cheer, and everyone made an effort to share in the general happiness. The very poor were invited to be their neighbours' guests, and when Shloach Monoth was sent in, they never let the plate go out empty—it always held a few tiny cakes, or a handful of bobies (large beans), and these were accepted by the well-to-do as if they had been expensive delicacies. The ones who could afford to send a piece of stuff for a dress, a fine cake or money, to the less fortunate, expected nothing in return but the little plate covered with a handkerchief so that no one should see what was inside, and took it in with expressions of delight. It was all a matter of neighbourly good-will; the larger gifts would have been worthless without it, and it made the small ones precious.

The white cloth was spread, the candles were lighted, the old and young men and some of the women and girls went to the Shool to listen to the Megillah of Esther. The boys waited—it was already getting dark, and they were eagerly expecting the return of Reb Mendel from Jaffa, whither he had driven that morning with some of the older girls and two of the boys, Abraham and Moses, who were to make purchases for themselves and for their families. All the money that could be saved through the winter by the women and girls, and most of the boys' Chanuka money, was kept for Purim to buy gifts and rattles and masks with. So when it grew dark and no waggon could be heard coming, not that it could be heard far off on the sandy road, there was no small anxiety as to where it might be.

What could have happened to the party?—they ought to have been back hours ago. It was no use, said the boys, going to Shool to hear the story of Esther if they had no rattles to shake at the mention of Haman. And then there were the masks for the play, which they were going to perform from house to house—how terrible it would be if they should be lost—the whole play would come to nothing. Some of the boys were taken to Shool without rattles, but it did not seem like Purim at all till supper-time. Then, when the boys saw the delicious Hamantaschen, stuffed with apple, cinnamon, and raisins, they forgot their anxiety about the waggon for the time being, and gave themselves up to enjoyment. Even a Purim supper, however, comes to an end. It was now quite dark, and there were no tidings of Reb Mendel and his waggon.

A few of the young men saddled their horses and rode out to seek the missing ones, taking a trumpet to blow if they should find them. They had just reached the outskirts of the Colony, when two little figures came in sight, hurrying towards them. These turned out to be Moses and Abraham, the two boys who had gone to town in the morning. They told the lads that Reb Mendel's waggon had broken down about half-an-hour's ride away, and as Reb Mendel could not leave the girls alone with the little boys, for fear of the Arabs, he had sent them on for help, and they had run nearly all the way. The young fellows blew three loud blasts on the trumpet, gave the boys a lift home, and soon a waggon was sent out to bring in the rest of the party and their purchases. When the Colony boys got hold of their rattles, they made such a noise that their elders were thankful when they got tired and went to bed.

Next morning they started masquerading, some as beggars with a big stick, a sack over their shoulders and very old shoes much too large for them; some as women with shawls over their heads and a large market-basket; others with the mask of an old Rabbi, long ear-locks and a kaftan.

They started at the head of the street, and went to the door of each house in turn, performing antics and singing songs, and then holding out their hands for a small gift in coin, which was never refused them. When they met a girl carrying a plate with a Purim gift to some one's family, they surrounded her at once, tried to pull the handkerchief off the plate to see what was underneath, snatch something, and run away to eat it, or insist on the girl giving them some money. If the girl resisted, there was a scuffle and screams, till some older person came out and interfered. But no child was ever punished for mischief at Purim, and, though the girls would get cross, they knew beforehand what to expect, and they liked taking the plates round, because they always received a few silver coins in reward. This money was kept for some special purpose.

That afternoon Miriam and Sarah were coming along, bound for the same house, when they noticed a group of little boys with their heads together behind the large barn.

"Let us go quietly up to them," said Sarah, "and find out what they are plotting together."

They approached the boys on tip-toe and looked over their shoulders. The boys were counting money and talking at the same time.

"We never enjoyed ourselves so much before," said Moses; "if Purim could only last! It is the only really good opportunity we get for turning tables on those girls. They are continually interfering with us and spoiling our plans."

"We shall spoil a few more yet!" said Miriam in a loud voice. The boys started in surprise.

"What did I say?" said Moses. "There they are again."

"What do you want?" asked Joseph.

"Nothing," replied Miriam; "only to see what mischief you were contriving together."

"If you thought we were up to mischief" returned Joseph, "you were quite mistaken, for we are simply counting up our gains."

"How much have you got?" asked Sarah,

sitting down beside him; "and what are you going to do with it?"

"One question at a time! We have got more than you, that much is certain."

"Is it?" said Miriam; and she put her hand into her pocket to make her coins jingle. "Listen! What a lot! and I have more at home."

"How much altogether. Tell us!" said the boys, now very curious.

"Tell me how much you have and I will tell you how much I have, Miriam and I together." Miriam and Sarah were inseparables—it was said they dreamt the same dreams of a night.

"Count, count, boys," said Abraham, who knew that Sarah was very determined, and that Miriam would keep her friend's secret, "and we will tell them how much we have."

The boys counted—it came to 10 francs and a little over.

"A very nice amount," said the girls, "and now what are you going to do with it?"

"We haven't settled yet," said the boys. "First we must take out 1s. 10d. for the poor, because our fathers say we should accustom ourselves to do this from childhood. That will leave us a franc a-piece and a few metalliks, about two metalliks each."

"We can buy a lot of green figs from the Arabs with that," said Chaim.

"And make ourselves as ill as we were after the melon?" said Dan. "Let us keep it for Passover, and then go out with the master and spend it in town."

"A good idea," said Joseph, "for we have cakes and sweets enough at home to last till then, and we shall save up our pocket-money and make it a little more."

"So that's settled, is it?" said Miriam. "Now, Sarah, what do you think of these boys who give themselves such airs and think themselves worth so much more than we are, and all they can think to do with their Purim money is to save it up for kosher sweets at Passover?"

The boys looked a little ashamed, but Moses said: "We earned it ourselves, and what wonderful thing could we do with a franc each? We may as well have a little enjoyment out of it."

"And what are you going to do with yours?" inquired the rest.

"Listen, boys," said Miriam. "You know the poor old woman with the little grandchildren to whom we gave the sack of corn? She never asks for anything; she always says she has enough, although she is so old and has to feed those children, which makes one the more anxious to help her. So all the winter some of the mothers and girls, those who had the time to spare, have been sewing and making clothes for her and the little ones, enough to last a whole year. We younger girls wanted to do something too, so we all settled to give our Purim money, and Sarah had a perfectly splendid idea : to bake a Hamantasche and put the money inside wrapped in paper, and lots of poppy-seed outside, so that the old woman should not suspect anything till she breaks it. And she will not know from whom the money comes, because there will be Hamantaschen from nearly everyone."

The boys stared with amazement. Chaim sat with his mouth open, imagining the old Granny with the Hamantasche, and no one knew what to say, for there was no doubt about it: the girls had shewn themselves brighter, cleverer, more generous than their brothers.

At length Abraham said : " I think the girls have done nobly, but then women are always supposed to know more about giving charity than men."

" Where is it written, 'O wise son of Israel ? ' " asked Miriam. " The Bible makes no difference between men and women, and so the boys should do like the girls, and share their good fortune with the poor."

" We will give you our Purim money," said Abraham, " to put into the Hamantasche. Let the poor old Granny and the children have a bit of pleasure for once. Of course our fathers would provide for them anyhow, but I heard mine say it would be rather a strain on the Colony, particularly as some more poor families are likely to be coming after the pogroms in Russia."

Chaim looked a little mournful because there would certainly be no green figs now, but now a boy held back, and all the money was put into Miriam's hands for the Hamantasche.

"I have another idea," said Sarah, anxious to make the most of this opportunity to influence the boys. "You know the savings-boxes for the poor and sick which our parents hang up in the house, and the box of Reb Baal Nesmeyer into which we have to drop something when we have recovered from an illness or escaped some misadventure? Well, why should not each of us have a little tin box all our own, into which we might put a coin every week when we have our pocket-money or after any extra bad behaviour? Then we should always have something to give if need were."

The boys looked at each other as much as to say: "Really, those girls are wonderful!"

"Good," said Dan; and all the others repeated after him: "Good, very good."

"I will tell you what more," said Sarah; "why not tell everyone who comes to the play this evening that the entrance is twopence, to be spent in a good cause? No one who has it with him will refuse, and the others can give it another time. They will never insist on knowing exactly what the good cause is to be."

"Splendid!" cried all the boys together. "We shall take a lot of money, and then we will divide it equally and start our own savings-boxes.'

"Boys," said Abraham, "let us shake hands with these girls and decide to admit them henceforward into our councils, for we have never thought of anything better among us all than these ideas of Miriam and Sarah."

The girls blushed with pleasure, hands were shaken all round, and then the meeting dispersed.

The play was a great success and the audience were delighted to pay the entrance fee, so that altogether it was a very joyous Festival.

END